Disclaimer: This is a fantasy, fictional story about a bee. It's not meant to reflect the actual physiology of bees - similar in idea to Dreamworks' Bee Movie in 2007. The point of the story is the message it portrays, not the particulars of bee physiology.

What Others Are Saying

— BOBBY LEWIS, CANREADS TORONTO BOOK REVIEW

Jenny Alexander's The Bee that Waved at Me is a lovely story about a little girl who has a chance encounter with a talking bee whose stinger is broken. Through her kindness, Sara helps the bee realize that he can still be useful despite his perceived flaws. This story will lift children's spirits as they navigate tough times in their own lives, offering a heartwarming glimpse into the relationship between Sara and the bee.

Readers will delight in watching how Sara's kindness blossoms into something even greater, inspiring the bee to help flowers bloom. The questions included after the story also serve as wonderful tools to help children reflect on similar situations and doubts in their own life. With some religious themes, this book is an excellent choice for Christian or Catholic children. It would be a great addition to Sunday school lessons that emphasize kindness, perseverance, and seeing the good in others.

The Bee that Waved at Me is a charming story with a message of resilience certain to resonate with young readers. Perfect for teaching children to embrace the things that make them different, this is a book that will remind little ones to be kind to themselves.

Dedication

I dedicate this book to Wren, Willa, and Forrest - my nieces and nephew. May you find your purpose early.

The bee waved at me. What a sight to see.

I stepped closer, thinking I imagined it.
The bee waved again. I decided to wave
back.

"Come closer, wee one," the bee said.

Wow, a bee that talks and waves! I took two more steps. Only two, because I couldn't get any closer.

"Do I look okay to you?" The bee spoke again.

I studied him from head to toe. He looked marvelous to me.

"You're part of God's beautiful creation."

A tear slid down the bee's face. "But my stinger doesn't work."

"That's okay. My uncle has to tape a bicycle horn to the outside of his car because the horn is broken. That doesn't stop him from driving."

"But bees are supposed to sting." The bee's voice dropped a little.

"They're also supposed to help plants get bigger and make food," I replied.

"I'm still doing those things."

"See! You still work — just like my uncle's car."

"But the facts haven't changed. I'm still broken," the bee said.

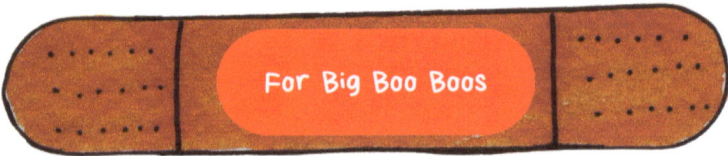

For Big Boo Boos

"Right before my birthday party last year, I broke my arm."

"I'm sorry," the bee replied. His little arm touched mine.

"I'm better now. Besides, it didn't stop me from having a party or going to school. Even if your stinger broke, you still help the plants."

The bee's head shot up. His eyes looked brighter.

"Thank you, wee one."

The bee's small mouth turned up at the corners.

"Do you feel better now?" I asked.

The bee nodded.

After that, he flew away.

He flew away so fast, I wondered if I imagined the whole thing.

The bee that waved at me. It happened! I didn't imagine it at all. I thought about Mr. Bee from morning until night.

I thought about him when I went to school.

BUSY BEE ELEMENTARY

I thought about him when I got in bed. I couldn't get Mr. Bee out of my head.

But as the months passed, the memory faded, and I didn't think about Mr. Bee quite so much. Life was normal, and I did the things I always did. For example, I read the Good Book every day.

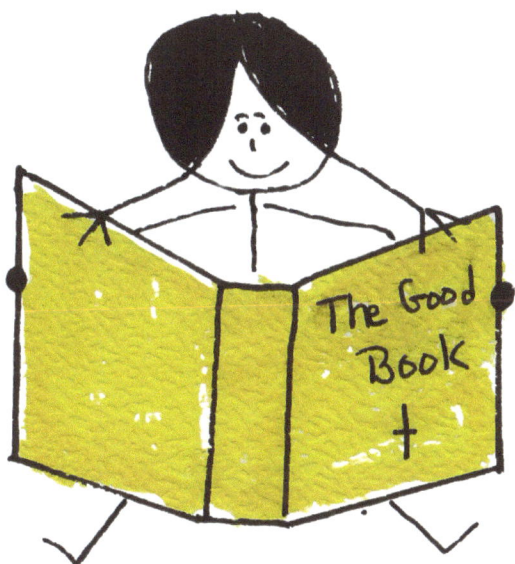

The Good Book

I finished school for the year.

I spent summer vacation playing outside with
my best friend.

I watched Tiny Tales on TV with mom and dad before bed every night.

Nothing was out of the ordinary all summer. But everything changed in early September Because one day after school something magical happened. I noticed a beautiful bush with pink heart-shaped flowers in my front yard that I never saw before.

The closer I got to them, the more they reminded me of my mom's perfume. I was mesmerized by the scent until suddenly, I heard it. The noise was so faint, I barely noticed it.

But I heard it a second time.

"Psst, wee one."

My head shot up. I was face to face with Mr.
Bee.

"Mr. Bee!!" I exclaimed. "The flowers are so beautiful. And I know you helped them grow."

He smiled the biggest I'd seen him smile yet. "You were right before. I work after all."

"I'm helping the flowers," he said with a sparkle in his eyes.

"I knew I'd see you again," I replied.

"And I knew I didn't imagine you. I only wondered for a tiny second."

"I'm no imaginary friend," Mr. Bee said.

Then, he winked at me. Yes, he really did!

Wow! A bee that winks, waves, and talks!

He winked once more, waved, and then flew away.

As I watched him go, I had no doubt about our encounter.

A few weeks later, I wrote about Mr. Bee and me. It was perfect for my school assignment.

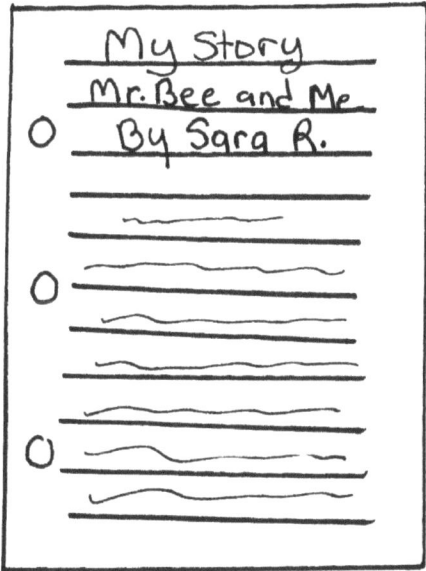

My Story
Mr. Bee and Me
By Sara R.

I got a good grade for being so imaginative.

I didn't imagine Mr. Bee but didn't bother to correct my teacher.

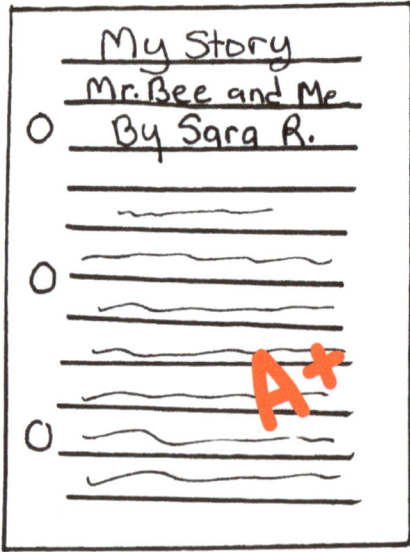

My encounter with him was just for me.

And his encounter with me was just for him.

That's exactly how it was meant to be.

Reflection Questions:

1. What kinds of things do you like to do?

2. What are you good at?

3. In what ways do you like to help others?

4. What kinds of things do you say to yourself? Are they mostly positive or mostly negative?

5. Use the space below to write down three to five positive things about yourself.

1.
2.
3.
4.
5.

Acknowledgments

Thank you to my husband, Curtis Alexander. Your support and input on this book were most helpful. You helped me believe I could illustrate it myself.

Thank you, Paige Spear, for your feedback on the manuscript. Your encouragement made a difference.

Thank you also to my sister-in-law Corrie Alexander. The brush pens you gave me for Christmas were perfect for the illustrations.

www.ingramcontent.com/pod-product-compliance
Lightning Source LLC
Chambersburg PA
CBHW041822040426

42448CB00026B/41